Coming Back a Millionaire

A true life mantra…

Winston Bear

Some thoughts to remind struggling entrepreneurs that if it was done it can be redone…

no white flags!

Where are you now?

Rebuild and Rebirth

From the Beginning

It started as a true American dream. Small town, dirt poor kid made good. White trash that carried water every winter so the trailer he shared with his Mom and brother had an in-door bathroom. No this wasn't the 30's this was the 70's and 80's. Hard work and dedication ended with a seven figure income.

I was mentored by a former FBI agent, man of God, and champion in life. He never had a hand out or gave freebees. I can remember when I was 8 asking him to buy me a calf. He said no and told me I could afford it on my own. I was dumbfounded, and only a kid. He took me to where my uncle was doing construction and I became the sweep up boy, go get it kid, and all around slave. I LOVED IT! By the end of the summer I bought my first calf.

So that I would never forget how hard it was to make the money, my mentor made me go pick that calf up every morning before school and walk it across the pen. When the calf became too heavy for me to carry we sold it and bought 2 more.

The same rules applied in my business. When the business became too heavy I got rid of the excess and at the end of the day I ultimately made more.

Turns on a Dime.

In the first year of marriage my wife suffered an aneurysm and brain surgery, but survived. She would suffer 5 strokes over the next 3 years as well as be hospitalized dozens of times. I had to turn my business over to managers/friends that I would have trusted my children with. We found out quick that MONEY changes everything for those who will never understand the dedication, stress, and base intelligence to create it.

Over the next 2 years, with the help of 2 corrupt state employees, and 3 dirty attorneys, these opportunists and failures at life destroyed the business and did their best to destroy us; even our children were not exempt from the attacks. I got text messages and phone calls asking for my minor daughters (even pictures of male genitals) who had been listed as prostitutes by the very people the local law enforcement was helping attack us. You got to love the internet!

When it was all said and done, we were homeless, had more than $25,000.00 in judgments against me for a payroll that was less than $2000.00 short (some of which by employees that were working for our competitors in a different part of the state for the same time they were awarded compensation, and others who did not work for that company at all), a judgment for $1.8 Million dollars for an employee that was picked up and admitted to writing checks to himself out of my account, in some cases even forging my name. Oh and the near $2 million dollar judgment came as the SAME ATTORNEY that represented him in the employee theft case came back and was able to get a judgment against me stating that the employee stealing from me was actually the owner of my company. Did I say that this attorney also sat on the city council?

I could go on and on to include my cop brothers kid stealing from us when we literally had nothing, to living on whatever cans we could find on the side of the road.

In the face of it all, over the last 36 months, thru hard work and a little swallowing some pride, we have come back. This book is the daily mantra that I preached to myself and some of the pictures I kept around in front of me. I know if you truly are a self-starter, and destined to be great it will help you too. Remember no war was every won by surrendering…***no white flags! EVER…***

Para mi Chula
Como Siempre

SUPER CHICKEN 1981

Meet SUPER CHICKEN. In the 5th grade an art teacher told me that I had to make a clay pot for a project. I told him that it wasn't challenging enough and that I wanted to make a super hero comic strip. After some negotiating I won the chance to do my project, my way. Super Chicken was born in 1981.

The teacher gave me an "F" on the project stating a chicken did not define the fearless nature of a super hero. My reply was not only foreshadowing a daring business man willing to take risks but a bit of a clown.

I told him SUPER CHICKEN was the bravest of all super hero's even braver than him. He attacked my statement telling me that I was mistaken to which I told him he was mistaken and asked him if he was brave enough to have a pecker on his face!

I got a trip to the office and after some heated negotiations with the 5th grade principle, an "A" on the project. An entrepreneur was born that day…..TRUE STORY.

"Necessity may be the mother of invention, but poverty is the GOD of creativity."

- 2011

The tank man of Tiananmen Square

This hung above my make-shift desk and a folded copy I carried with me from 2011 to 2013.

This man faced those without integrity, cowards, liars, and thieves of dreams. This man is my hero, and short of Jesus Christ and my childhood mentor, is the bravest man I have ever seen.

"When you are attacked by those who will never amount to anything but still find time to slander your name, remember the tank man. Look at his picture, he is holding a white bag, not a white flag...Never give in, never give up...EVER."

"I have been poor, but I have never been broke."

- 2013

Two quick stories.

#1

When I was is college a professor made us write a paper on the most successful segment of society. The project had no length requirements or back-up; just original thought.

The next day all of came in and round tabled the question as a class. Physicians, lawyers, judges, stock brokers, all the professions you would expect. At the end we all were told the assignment was going to be thrown out as we all had failed. He said the answer we were looking for was a by-choice homeless street person.

Dumbfounded we questioned his logic. We were all astonished when he proved that all of us looked forward to the day when we did not have a boss, would much rather get up at 10AM than 6AM, drink when we want, smoke if we want, not pay taxes and have no responsibilities. It was a laughable thought until he validated the following mathematical scenario:

> The average guy begging on a busy corner with get 10 cars and hour to give him a dollar.
> If he works 12 hours that's $120.00 per day.
> If he works a 6 day work week that's $720.00 per week
> 52 weeks per year is $37,440. Annual income.

Now here is the rub:

If you have a salary of $40,000.00 per year, you should bring home around $34,000.00 per year. Now let's put some reality with that:

Annual Income after taxes:	$34,000.00
Cost of Rent:	$7200.00
Cost of Car Payments:	$3600.00
Cost of Fuel:	$2500.00
Cost of Clothes for Work :	$1800.00
Cost of Maintenance:	$2000.00
Cost of Utilities:	$3600.00
Cost of Cell Phone:	$700.00

OK STOP THERE…

Balance Sheet:

Homeless GUY

Annual Income:	$37,440.00
Income after annual expenses:	$37,440.00

Now YOU	
Annual Income:	$40,000.00
Income after annual expense:	$12,600.00

REALLY MAKES YOU CONSIDER A LIFE ON THE STREET!!!

#2

I had the fortunate pleasure of working for Chuck Norris as a Martial Arts instructor for inner city kids. Mr. Norris makes champions out of those kids who would never have been told there was a tiger inside them and not a mouse. Through the dedication of some outstanding individuals, the organization has touched thousands of kids. Kids that would otherwise be a statistic or an obituary headline. ***If you are ever looking for a worthy organization to put your money look up Chuck Norris and his Kick Start program.

During my time in the Norris organization were learned and drilled 2 things into our students and each other.

1. **Winning is not a sometime thing winning is an all the time thing, unfortunately, so is losing. –From the incomparable Vince Lombardi.**

2. **To me the most important:** Mr. Norris was asked in an interview what it was like on his rise to the top when he lost a match. His reply has been my personal mantra, and it should be yours as well…Mr. Norris said, (para phrased) I have never lost a match; I have been behind on points and ran out of time but never lost. And those points my opponents got were not a loss either, only training points that improved me as an athlete. Because the next time they tried them they would not score.

Take a page from Chuck Norris book!

"I have homeless but never hopeless."

- 2013

"I only couldn't fly because I believed in gravity more."

- 2013

Gravity is a lie. Just as those who will tell you that your business will fail and that you are worthless. Remind those people of Orville and Wilber Wright. To that end just call them Orville, don't tell them why just call them Orville. Don't worry they won't figure it out. This will be our private joke.

PROCRASTINATION

"I believe tomorrow I will master the art of procrastination, because today I have too much on my schedule."

- 2013

You won't always win...

"Be strong enough to get F¡#@*!, but never forget how bad it felt. Truly a learning experience."

- 2013

Questions…….

"If it is going to be an if don't do it. You're the boss make a decision and role with the punches."

- 2013

"The trash will be protected by the law at every level."

- 2010

If you have not had the pleasure yet, you will. While your focused on growing your business, the ass-clowns that have been fired, not hirable, or even some really dumb ones that still work for you will toil tirelessly to do harm to you and your venture.

I have a theory that those that will never have anything see it as a badge of honor to bring harm to those who work their butts off to become the best that they can be. Unfortunately, just like the old adage says, "the greasy wheel gets the grease", these individuals will illicit law enforcement, work force commissions, the IRS, regulatory bodies, and every agency with an acronym to stop your progress.

Going in to these daily distractions, know, you competition has these problems too, and to the best of your ability focus these idiots towards your competitors as potential new hires for their organization.

Because if they were screw ups for you, they will be screw ups for them and you already know how it is going to end.

"Let your disappointments pile up into the mountain that you will one day stand on top of as a success."

- 2013

"I never understood peace until I had seen war."

- 2013

Prepare every day for the battle.

"Practice does not make perfect, perfect practice makes perfect."

- 1985

stamina

As a former athlete I know a little something about stamina. There are all kinds of tricks and supplements you can use to help you take that extra step. But what matters the most is emotional stamina.

When they hurl the names, accusations, and even the ridiculous at you, your temptation will be to fight back. Meet them in the middle we always said.

I tell you this now, when you pull off task to meet in the middle, you allow not only your pride to get involved, you let your competitor move forward. Stay focused.

There was a group of individuals in my company that were stealing, abusing other employees, lying, scheming, all led by a wanna-be preacher. Their most favorite quote was that they would not stop attacking me unless I was dead or in prison, no matter what they had to do. Let me tell you, they broke laws, lied to federal officers, hacked emails, stole my identity, set my home up with multiple moving agencies, and more unspeakable craziness. Three years later they are all in the same place in life; have moved onto attack other companies while we have witnessed recovery thru hard work. By not engaging them at their level, and keeping our eyes on the prize we were able to stand again, and you will too.

There is a great commercial of an athlete riding into town on a bus and the windows getting pelted with raw eggs as crowds screamed at him. When he got off the bus he put on his head set to walk thru the crowd of screaming evilness. He cranked his music and pictured the win in his mind, never hearing the negative words being hurled at him.

Later that evening after he realized the win, he watched the same crowd attacking their own team as he walked away in peace, satisfied and content that he performed his best and won.

Don't focus on the distractions.

The Boar Hog theory of worries:

"Worrying is worthless as tits on a boar hog."

\- 1975 My Grandpa

Boar hogs were made as powerful and aggressive creatures. If you have ever hunted one you know that they are basically fearless. It may sound funny but you need to see yourself as a boar hog.

Thoughts

In closing of this first set of ideas on business and entrepreneurship, I would like to throw at you some final thoughts.

- ➢ Your most basic need is employees, which are also your biggest problem. They are going to steal, they are going to lie.

- ➢ A good friend once told me that he hires people with the understanding that he goes into the arrangement knowing that he is just waiting for the moment they disappoint him. It is unfortunately going to be the one you have placed the most trust in as a leader in your team.

- ➢ Your greatest asset is not that rock star employee; it is that carnivorous drive in your gut.

- ➢ Build a business around an employee and you will one day hand it over to him, either voluntarily are by force.

- ➢ Know your competitor as well as yourself. Know his home life, his church, his pants size, everything.

- ➢ Don't go into a negotiation until you have fought that battle 11 times in your mind. You must have won before the discussions begin.

- ➢ Never, never, never give up. That doesn't mean you won't have to back up and punt but you should never give up the fight.

- ➢ No White Flags…Ever.